tethered

A.C. Sol

Presentation by *BookLeaf Publishing*

Web: www.bookleafpub.com

E-mail: info@bookleafpub.com

ISBN: 978-93-95784-62-7

First edition 2022

To my nineteen year-old self:

It's happening!

ACKNOWLEDGEMENT

My thanks to BookLeaf for this amazing writing challenge with the opportunity to publish. You've made one little person's dream come true to have published something in their lifetime.

To my Yin, you fuel my bravery. Your love, support and encouragement is something I will continue repaying in this lifetime.

PREFACE

"Tied to my heart like a kite to a string" were the lyrics from Star that hit home.

These words stayed with me, wrapped in a melody that understood my heartache and grief. In my minds eye, my heart really was still tethered to a person and life I had known for years. Could you know it? This feeling tethered to someone, while simultaneously working hard to release all that is holding you back?

In all honesty, I would not consider myself a poet - just someone who would jot down words and sentences here and there - in fleeting moments when my emotions felt raw. When the numbness from self preservation bent its knee to the weight of my new reality, I would turn to my little app and make use of it like my new-age diary. That may be why there are a handful of untitled pieces. My nature wishes they were titled, but they felt complete without.

I have always been a lover of words; of storytelling in any capacity. In movie quotes, musical lyrics, anecdotes from dear friends - I hold these words close. They have been imprinted into my soul; tethered is a love letter to myself and my life. This writing challenge came at the right time. I had wanted to challenge myself despite the intimidation; I would showcase my words, thoughts, and feelings on paper. I am both self-conscious in this vulnerability, and self-congratulatory in that my desire to challenge myself also resulted in fulfilling a dream.

I will leave you with another favourite quote of mine:

"I want to be like water. Strong enough to hold up a ship, yet slip through your fingers." - Dawson's Creek

How can you find your
own way
when you feel tethered
to someone?

why is loneliness
so loud

I always thought
I was the sun
But I was the shadow
who would not leave
your side

Insomnia

They say you fall asleep faster beside the one
you love...

My body already knew
what my heart
wouldn't admit.

There was no love
for me here.

Your days are full
but are they fulfilling

single

That's almost one letter
for every year we were
together.

I guess the heartbreak is silent

when you kissed me
I felt the universe quiver

Affection is greater than
perfection
I mistook your silences for
indifference
But you felt these silences as our souls
speaking

I was so busy being in love

that I stopped loving myself.

Cherry Blossoms

I didn't know I was
holding my breath until
you left

And then suddenly,
I was me again

goldilocks

Your first love says all the right things.
All.
The.
Right.
Things.
They say things just right - and then, you learn
from that.

Your next love awakens something in you;
they kiss you the way you want to be kissed.
They kiss you just right - and then you learn
from that.

And so,
this next one ...
Your next one will love you the way you've been
craving.
They'll love you just right - and if you're lucky,

They'll love your body, mind, and soul
Just.
Right.
And you will continue on, learning with each
other.

Vent/ricle

Why do we say
They took our heart with them; or
They are my heart; or
They stole my heart

As if the heart isn't an organ?

My answer?

It is because I was very aware of my own
heart beat when you were around.

How quick.
How calm.
How soothed.
How at home it hummed.

You only need me when it's raining

You only find me
when it's raining

Yet still my heart
shelters you

Mars vs. Venus

I found reasons to
stay

You found reasons to
leave

The End.

11:11 Yin

When I say "I miss you"
I don't just mean I miss us
being in the same room together.

What I mean is

I miss you, in the way you bring value to my
consciousness

I miss you, in the way the moonlight comforts
the soul

I miss you, in the way we yearn through a
memory.

I miss you, best friend.

la petite mort

man or woman
it's all the same
still feeling numb
so I'm to blame
for seeking out flesh
and their distracting warmth
to distract me from your name

Lost / Lust

Oh,
it's
You.

One stroke away from !

la petite mort ii

I don't make love
I make poetry
imprint your words on my flesh
immortalize my pleasure

I'll write you love letters inside your thighs
Reward your submission
Crush your inhibitions
as you beg
for that little death

I must have really loved you

They say emotional trauma results in memory
loss.
Suppressing emotion affects memory.

In my haste to forget you,
I seem to have become forgetful.

loveseat freestyle one

They're preaching patience
You're a work in progress
Count your blessings
This life shit ain't obvious
We're in the Wild West,
the land of the lawless
Make good impressions
What's today's mathematics?
Minus the menace
Taking the L's
Life Lessons
Words are weapons
Shoot shots like a Wesson
Throw dubs on the beat
and I kill'em
Pursuit in knowledge
but I feel like a hostage
Know thy self,
hard to break out of bondage
Fight to survive
Afraid of feeling like cattle
So how I fight is
lyrically going to battle

four chambers, five letters

Just know that as I pick up the pieces
I can rearrange them in a way that is less

fragile

More spiritual
More compassionate
More harmonic
More at home in my flesh and in awe of my
resilient chambers.

www.ingramcontent.com/pod-product-compliance
Lightning Source LLC
Chambersburg PA
CBHW060928130726
48001CB00006B/2466